Mishu the little monkey had ten brothers and
sisters. They lived with their mum and dad
in the gardens of the Taj Mahal.

Mishu thought the Taj Mahal was amazing. He loved the big white dome, the four tall towers and the beautiful pool.

The pool had fountains! Mishu loved to run past the fountains as they shot up into the air.

The Top of the Taj Mahal

Written by Narinder Dhami

Illustrated by Anaïs Goldemberg

Introduction

The Taj Mahal is a very famous building in India. Lots of people visit it every day.

OXFORD
UNIVERSITY PRESS

OXFORD
UNIVERSITY PRESS

Great Clarendon Street, Oxford, OX2 6DP, United Kingdom

Oxford University Press is a department of the University of Oxford.
It furthers the University's objective of excellence in research, scholarship,
and education by publishing worldwide. Oxford is a registered trade mark
of Oxford University Press in the UK and in certain other countries

British Library Cataloguing in Publication Data
Data available

ISBN: 978-0-19-835644-8

10 9

Paper used in the production of this book is a natural, recyclable product
made from wood grown in sustainable forests. The manufacturing process
conforms to the environmental regulations of the country of origin.

Printed in China by Shanghai Offset Printing Products Ltd

Acknowledgements

Series Advisor: Nikki Gamble
Illustrated by Anaïs Goldemberg
Designed by Fiona Lee, Pounce Creative

One day, Mishu's brothers and sisters
were playing hide-and-seek in the trees.
"Can I play?" asked Mishu.

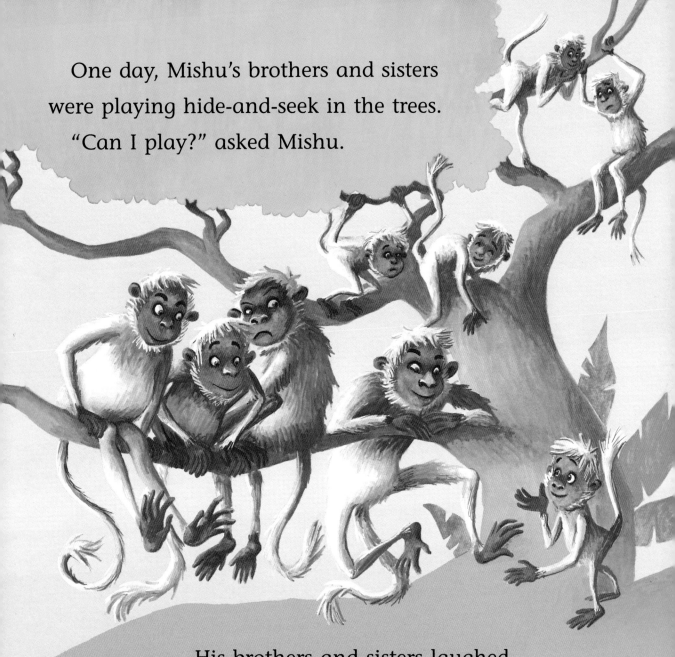

His brothers and sisters laughed.
"You can't climb as high as we can,"
they said. "You're too *small!*"

Mishu stared sadly at his brothers and sisters.
They never let him join in with their games.

"I can climb higher than all of you!" boasted Mishu. "And I'm going to climb to the top of the Taj Mahal!"

"You are a silly little monkey. The Taj Mahal is too big to climb!" said Mishu's brothers and sisters. And they ran off, swinging from tree to tree.

Mishu went to find his best friend, Kojo the parakeet.

"I'm going to climb to the top of the Taj Mahal!" Mishu told Kojo.

Kojo was amazed!

"But the Taj Mahal is as high as the sun in the sky!" she squawked.

"I'm still going to try," Mishu said.
"Will you come with me?"

Kojo flapped her wings. "Of course I will," she replied.

Let's go!

So Mishu and Kojo set off through the gardens to the Taj Mahal.

"Are you off to climb the
Taj Mahal, Mishu?" his
sisters teased.

"You need wings, like Kojo," shouted his brothers.
"Then you can *fly* to the top!"
And they all burst out laughing.

"I'll show *you!*"
Mishu cried.

The Taj Mahal was closed that day. The fountains had been turned off and the pool was clear and still.

Mishu could see the reflection of the Taj Mahal in the water.

12

Mishu and Kojo went up to the
Taj Mahal. It was taller than the tallest
tree in the gardens. It looked bigger
and bigger as they got closer and closer.

Suddenly Mishu felt very small and scared.
He took a deep breath ...

Mishu tried to jump onto the wall
of the Taj Mahal. But the white stone
was very smooth and very shiny,
so Mishu just slid down the wall.

"Try again, Mishu," Kojo called. "But be careful."

Mishu tried again. And again. But every time, he slid back down.

"You're a brave monkey, Mishu," said Kojo. "But the wall is too smooth and shiny to climb."

"I need another plan," said Mishu.

Mishu sat down and thought for a while.

"I've got it!" cried Mishu. "Kojo, will you fly me to the top of the Taj Mahal?"

"Of course!" Kojo replied. "Grab on to my legs and don't let go!"

Mishu held on to Kojo's legs with his paws.
At last, he was going to the top of the Taj Mahal!

Kojo flapped her wings but she and Mishu didn't
fly up into the air. Kojo flapped her wings harder
and harder but nothing happened.

Finally, Kojo gave up.

"You're too heavy for me, Mishu!" Kojo panted.

"Thank you for trying to help," Mishu said sadly.

"I'll never get to the top of the Taj Mahal now!"
sighed Mishu.

Mishu and Kojo walked home in silence.

On the way, they passed the pool.

Mishu noticed the reflection of the Taj Mahal in the water again. This time, it gave him a wonderful idea!

"Kojo, will you go and find my brothers
and sisters?" Mishu asked. "Tell them
I'm on top of the Taj Mahal!"

Kojo looked puzzled. "But you're *not!*" she squawked.
"Just go and tell them!" laughed Mishu.

Kojo didn't know what Mishu was up to.
But she flew off and found Mishu's
brothers and sisters playing in the trees.

"Come quickly," Kojo called.
"Mishu is on top of the Taj Mahal!"

"He *can't* be!" the monkeys gasped.

The monkeys followed Kojo to the pool.
Mishu was standing on one of the fountains.

"Look at me!" Mishu yelled. "I'm on top of
the Taj Mahal!"

But Mishu's brothers and sisters just looked
very confused.

"But you're *not* on top of the Taj Mahal!"
said one of Mishu's brothers.

"Oh yes, I am!" said Mishu, grinning. "Look at the water!"

The fountain was right on top of the reflection of the Taj Mahal!

Everyone began to laugh.

"What a clever little monkey you are, Mishu," said his brothers and sisters. "You and Kojo can join in with our games from now on!"

"No," Mishu laughed. "You can join in with *our* games!"